The Whisper,
The Storm and The Light
In Between

The Whisper,
The Storm and The Light
In Between

CLARA OLIVO

ALEGRIA
PUBLISHING

davina@alegriamagazine.com

Library of Congress Control number: 2022906338

ISBN: 9798986084404

Published by Alegria Publishing
Book cover and layout by Carlos Mendoza

Clara, your voice can be both, storm and whisper.
Your poetry is the light in between- JPR

CONTENTS

Foreword
by josh martinez

This is a work of discovery. Depending on who you are, the word "discovery" can have different meanings. Like "exploration," there's a power dynamic hidden within. Who has the power to explore? Why do we always center the point of view of the explorer? Why has exploration throughout history led to exploitation? People often use "exploration" in the context of the unknown. One example: white settlers "explored" the American West as if nobody had ever before lived there.

The term "discovery" is closer to unearthing something rare, something splendid. We discover things that are already there. If a tree goes undiscovered in a forest, does it really exist? Of course, it does!

The poems you are about to read contain moments of self-discovery. Clara is like many people born during Reagan's America. We come from a cultural experience of suppression and oppression. How could we not be shaped by that? People who feel different in a society risk defining themselves by what they are not, rather than what they are. White supremacy culture demands that we minimize our differences unless they're profitable. For those of us outside the norm, it's a lifelong practice to discover who it is we really are.

In *The Whisper, The Storm and The Light In Between*, Clara shares with us discovery through her storytelling. These are stories of refusal, reclamation, and liberation. Clara reveals discoveries about her history and the history of her ancestors. Discoveries of the history, written in flesh, of the country that her family once called home. The horrific discovery, like that of a cancer, of the forces that conspired to erase her AfroSalvadoran identity.

When I think about discovery, I wonder about its context. Who is discovering whom? Who is worthy of telling their stories? Who is worthy of receiving them? What radiant existence did something have before it was "discovered"?

Amid the discovery in these pages is a truth. *We*, the reader, are discovering *her*. We are witness to her legacy. The legacy of all the people who came before her. Before there were such a thing as immigrants or even borders. We discover the legacy of Clara's ancestors through Clara. The legacy that others have tried to diminish or devalue. We discover Clara saying, gently, fiercely: I discovered myself. I lived before you knew me. I live, even to this day. I live on in these words and in your discovery of them. There she is, en voz clara, diciendo "mira no más. Aquí estoy."

Look no more. Here I am.

A Message from the Author

Beloved reader,
This book was never meant to exist. The words and histories tied to my existence have been repeatedly removed, erased, stolen, white-washed, and lost. An entire history that exists within my bloodline, spanning two continents and a middle passage.

As an Afro-Salvadoreña in diaspora, reclaiming my identity and roots has been an arduous, life-affirming practice. El Salvador is a country devoid of Blackness. That is, there are no Black people in El Salvador— or that is what many Salvadoreños will tell you, because they firmly believe this to be true.

Unbeknownst to me and mine, enslaved Africans were brought to El Salvador in the sixteenth century. Their presence and fate tied to the horrors of colonization in America Central. In El Salvador, slavery was banned in 1825, making it the third country to abolish slavery in the Americas after Haiti and Chile.

The violent, anti-Black myth originated after an immigration law was enacted in 1933 by Dictator Maximiliano Hernandez Martinez. It ordered to prohibit the entry of African descended people (among other non-Europeans) into El Salvador.

No one in my family was made aware of these facts despite my father being Black, born and raised in Sonsonate, and donning the ubiqui-tous nickname for many melanated bichos y hombres, *Negro.*

The influence of the African diaspora is prevalent in even the deepest aspects of Salvi culture. From our sopa de pata to the marimba, our African roots are buried deep in our native land and rippled in our heritage. Yet the denial of Blackness supersedes these contributions and realities, displacing an entire people from themselves. My lived experience is not unique; my story is not my own. For so long, I be-lieved I was the only one, and nobody would understand the crush-ing identity crisis that came from living in diaspora without even knowing what the word meant or that it could apply to me despite all the proof I was surrounded with.

When I think about it all and line up the pieces, everything falls into place. I finally understood that I was never meant to feel this way because I was never meant to be here. I was never meant to be displaced. My people were never meant to be colonized in 1492, never meant to be enslaved and dragged across the Atlantic in 1526. We were never meant to survive La Matanza in El Salvador in 1932, or endure the U.S.- sanctioned Civil War that forced my family to migrate in the first place.

White supremacy has settled into our land and bore a strange fruit we've forcibly consumed. Like lambs to the slaughter unknowingly gorging on our last meal, I ate up the lies the American Dream served. I tirelessly tried to fit into the idealistic norms never intended for me or people like me. I became immersed in American culture because as a child of immigrants, I *had* to do better than them. I *had* to reach further than they ever could and break through every door that was slammed in their faces. To do this, I had to assimilate so I could better navigate this new home they found themselves in all the while, never looking inward or back to see why we had to do these things in the first place.

The Whisper, The Storm and The Light in Between is an exploration of my lifetime, the history of my lineage, and the myriad of disasters that led me to where I am today. The Whisper son los poemas echoing from my moments of silent suffering. The words I didn't have that would help me understand and name the chaos around me. The Storm carries rage and ferocity against the disaster. It is the call to action in emphatic prose and the fury that comes from surviving life in the eye of the hurricane and finally having the voice and agency to speak to the lingering destruction. Amongst the rolling clouds looming overhead and the thunderclap of oppression felt throughout the atmosphere, Light breaks through to shine its warmth onto you. Lightning breaks between the dark, guiding you to strength and the power of hope. The light you need to guide you to your truest self.

A connection has been severed, and through poetry, a deep analysis of oppressive systems, and continuous reflection, I strive to mend the fabric of our tattered truth. The part nearest and dearest to me, with all the blistering intersections my ancestors have crossed, that led me to write this book before you.

I write this book during an interesting time in our history. As I type these words, many like mine are currently being burned and banned across the "united states". Poetry books, memoirs, and graphic novels are being pulled from school libraries in an attempt to erase the very history we embody. Unattainable to the future generations that are to shape and lead our world. How easy it is for me to say that this cultural genocide is intentional. Sadly, it's even easier for me to be silenced for saying so.

As I type, I fear this book will be banned for speaking the truth. Denunciando la injusticia de nuestro gobierno and the exploitation of our motherlands. I also fear that this book will never make it far and wide to amplify our realities. There are many external factors that continue to challenge and oppress my efforts, manifesting in mental illness, genetic disease, and a lack of generational wealth.

I occupy a body born of two lands, bound together in iron and blood lost in the deep blue sepulcro of the sea. I am a poet by heart and warrior incarnate, embracing the opportunities that survival has afforded me. I hold and share the knowledge and wisdom my ancestors and elders have saved despite all odds. It is what I hope to share with you through these poems as we explore the ever-changing landscape of time.

This much I know is true: words are powerful and capable of transforming everything we touch. I believe we all deserve to heal and be held by our community and kin, even during the most intangible of times. These poems are for you to remember that you are not alone. To remind you, beloved reader, that you are part of something greater. Our fears and fate are intertwined, and here we find ourselves together at last. Collective liberation, healing, and self-love require us to lean into one another to repair and reclaim what is truly ours. Poetry has the power to do exactly that.

The stories within these pages have traveled across time and space to reach you. It is only by our hard-earned resilience and ancestral strength we find ourselves here, in community. In lak'ech.

Follow the lines of the past and they will show you the way to the future. Between every sentence lies the truth of your connection to the land. To the struggle. To the light.

Con amor y gratitud,
Clara

CHAPTER 1

The Whisper

Birdsong

How do you move through the world
mija?
You belong everywhere
You belong nowhere
This is your home
Call it by any other name
America
Turtle Island
Abya Yala
And yet it still smells as sweet
Here is where
we wait for your return
Porque mira mi niña
*The world is **yours** and*
if they won't give it back
Then burn those mother fuckers down
With your words
your fight
your fury and
Reclaim your right
to belong

Metric

Her days were measured by grief.
Before she was born, she inherited the pain of genocide.
Imperialism is real and displacement is in her blood.

The warmth within her mother's womb
held the memories of survival.
Nine months she rested, suspended in the silence
of her ancestors.

Grief knocked again upon the wall, and the silence overcame
innocence lost. The image of her sister's naked body,
cold and lifeless, forever burned in her mind's eye.

She once spoke of the woman in white who asked for her soul
in her dreams and in the darkness that swallows the sun whole.
From then on, she knew she was meant to run.

And the race to the other side,
where the grass is said to be greener,
bared more poison than the fruit on our tainted land.
It isn't my mother's fault that displacement is in *my blood.*
She begins to grieve her own life
before she's even started to live.

Where Does It Come From (They Ask SO Casually)

My creativity flows from the world around me
The things I see when I close my eyes...
The hugs and hits that came from being
the youngest of four in a home of tortured souls
Survivors of our own undeserved hell
The sounds of screams for attention
over the deafening beat of the 8 am cumbias that fueled
my tired mami's soul as she cleans the mess from the night before
because *cleanliness is next to godliness* and here we practice
leave no trace
The inescapable sounds of celebration and pain
that only colonized people can bring
when singing of survival and glee
Before we learned the words and names of
displacement

                                              and *diaspora*

That bitter-sweet taste of freedom
como el mango verde de mi juventud
The forbidden fruit of knowledge picked too early
Melting forgotten memories onto my tongue
tastebuds rejoicing at the delicious surrender
as the *jugito de limón* dripssss down my lipssss
Glistening my chin leaving a story that only my skin can tell
The growing pains that came with always wanting to fit in
E x p a n d I n g/retracting
back (and forth) into the bite-size shape of my younger body but
There is no space for youth here!
They've stayed behind!

Locked in the room of their memories where movement stays hidden
and discovery of self lays quiet and deep in the slumber of depression
Where songs by boy bands and Slipknot
built the loudest walls that kept them silent and safe
Waking up to the glory of reflection
Rising to the opportunity to feel and reclaim
the message mis ancestros left hidden in the rain
Father Sky's sacred tears descend upon my face dripping truth
every drop rolling down onto the ground watering
the buried seeds the colonizers unwittingly planted
My words rising with the bittersweet blooms
Blessing me with hopes for a future I may never see
A hope that moves me to speak ancestral truth
May you hear it loud
May you know it well
Because in this truth is a history
you were never meant to hear

Playtime

Clarita grew up quiet and afraid
Heard that she was just too much sometimes
Put in the corner for talking out of turn
Talking back out of curiosity
perceived as disrespect
The wild child running up
and down the parking lot
Descalza y mechuda
Smaller than the boys who
kept her on her toes
Except that one time
they trapped her in the alley
Watched her struggle, scream and shout
Their Doberman biting at her bony legs
Like the chew toys it's been denied
Shock, awe and laughter paralyzing her until
Their familiar whistles beckoned their dog over
No blood dripping down
just bite marks she'd have to hide
Because snitches get stitches and lil homie just wanted to fit in
Feel loved and accepted
Is this not how we make friends?

Glock

The first time I held a gun was in first grade.
My friend, Cindy, lived across the way and went to the same
school I did.
Her long hair was to her waist. Mine would never compare, but we
tried.
Her big brother, Patrick, would play with the other big boys from
our
complex.
He was the nice one, never teasing me or trying to hurt me.
I don't remember why, or if I knew it was there,
hiding in the kitchen drawer, the second one from the top of the counter.

It was heavy and cold,
dark metal and brown grip
my six-year-old hands could barely wrap around.
Have you ever held anyone at gunpoint?

They tell you not to keep your guns in easy-to-reach places,
but I only remember this in English-language TV commercials.
I didn't fire it, I don't know if it was loaded.
I just remember playing cops and robbers in the parking lot of our
apartments
and the look in Patrick's eyes as I told him to *freeze*,
and the gun no longer within my reach.

Pobrecita Huerfanita

When I was little, after my father abandoned me, I became incredibly distressed, my first major loss in life. My family uses laughter to cope with trauma. In an attempt to make me feel better, some would make light of my cries and respond with a little song they made up, Pobrecita Huerfanita. This phrase encapsulates the complicated feelings and unresolved trauma surrounding the absence of my father. And so much more...

The times I want to call you
        when the nostalgia hits
The need for tender love and care
that only a father could bring
I stop in my tracks
Think back...   back...
When pre-k Clara needed you to pick her up after school
(because mama was working late, cleaning her 4th house of the day in the beautiful Hollywood hills)
When 8-year-old Clara lost her big sister (her best friend)
Y adonde estabas?
Espera, no importa
You never stepped up or in the times that it mattered
So why should I?

Oh...
There was that one time
One time
When Clara in her early 20's flew from Houston to L.A.
The day after mama passed away
I don't remember how she got your number
but I do remember saying
"Mama is gone... se murio"
The static crackling through the words
You made me repeat them
and despite the interference
and bad reception
My words became your new reality

Loud and clear
You said you would come
Crossing mountains and highways to be there for me
And mira no más, there you were
Ready to receive me in your arms
Pressing all the pain and disbelief out of me

The TLC that I know
only a dad can bring
That moment of stillness
of relief
I knew it wouldn't last

Because the day of the funeral
you said you would be there
And for a moment I believed it until
Pre-K Clara tugged at my arm
Reminding me that she's still waiting to get picked up
And 8-year-old Clara's stoic little face
Reminds me that you can't show your sadness
                              you gotta be strong

And just like that
We put down the phone
And we put you away
                    until

the next time

Birthday Cake

Mami confronted me in the car.
She's saying that tía Viqui was shocked
and appalled at how I ate my slice so fast.
Que vergüenza *hartándote* todo de un sólo.
Except I don't remember eating it all in one bite,
but I do remember being so ashamed
I didn't eat cake in front of anyone again.

The Illusionist

I hide my shame beneath my sweaters, hoping not to offend.
I was taught that this body, the ones like mine with lonjitas y panza
Son unas de las cosas más feas que puedes tener
(nadie te va a querer).
How the belly hangs over pubis and delicately folds
(not even I would want to hold).
Sucking you in with slim-fitting tights cutting circulation leaving traces
of shame imprinted on the tender brown skin I keep hidden within.
Pale by comparison and far away from judgmental eyes and fatphobic
spite,
starving you for attention, erasing parts of me that make me whole.
Hiding in plain sight underneath clothing that overflows.
People be praising my disappearance, acting like it's magic before their
eyes.
Never questioning why my sleight of hand tricks delivered desired
results
for the spectators of my show. It's tragic.
The real trick was being fooled into believing
I was ever the problem to begin with.

Face/off

Borderline,
but it's not my personality.
Teetering and tottering
in a world that is my own
and that which was constructed.
Ni de aquí ni de allá.
It can change any day.
Every moment a gift to be unraveled.
(Mis)understood.
Smile and wave,
keep up face.
Stomach churning,
full body aches.
And the sunshine calls me
but I can't move.
Executive dysfunction,
paralizada.
It begins at home.
My Tia says
It runs in the family.
I agree and say
"trauma is hereditary".
Indecisive, indistinguishable,
off/on/off in the blink of an eye,
fight/flight.
Mostly fawn when shit goes down,
she's been running for so long.
It's in the symptoms, they tell a story.
Homegirl just wants to let the world see
Smile and wave,
while I save face
so that I can face
another day.

Torn

My scars tell the story of my angst.
They are visible, and some are faded. But still,
my scars are the roadmap of my survival.
The twists and turns I had to take to find my way,
cutting through the burden of feeling
everything around me falling apart.

I used to hide them with long sleeves,
keep my secret to myself and away from prying eyes.
My scars turned me into the greatest liar you ever met,
hiding the truth of who I am and the battles I had to fight.

You see the depth of sorrow in the skin I'm in,
the traces of triumph over the unimaginable.
Unfathomable monsters I had to keep at bay,
wrestling demons and finding them a place to stay.

Quiet,
where no one will find them,
no one will question,
no one will know.
The monsters that dwell inside me trying to get out,
clawing their way through.

My skin bleeds the indigo mourning
of a displaced death from the inside out.
I bury my face into my pillows,
suffocating the anguish and my cries.

In solitude no one can hear you scream.
In quiet isolation no one can see you bleed.
In truth, no one can see you
until after the damage has been done.

A Love Letter to the Biggest Asshole I've Ever Known

Joey
Paquito
José

The child in the pictures
sitting at the front
criss-cross applesauce
Bowl-cut bangs
hanging over your brows
with a smile that can melt anyone
to your feet
Your cunning and your grace
Bestowed from the maternal embrace
of she who held us in her womb
With the stories and
legends of a people
you left behind

What was it like for you,
dear brother,
to come here so young and face
a big new world
What was it like, tiny butterfly
to undergo metamorphose
forcefully evolve
from the innocent child
with the mischievous smile
to the majestic man
who towered over many
Inciting the simultaneous fear and joy
your presence proposed

Your destiny carved and cut
by the world around you
The systems that'd trap you
in their deadly web
Spinning the lies
of freedom and equality
The American dream
                          we saw
on the (silver) screen
where men like you
died
trying to make that dream
come true

I knew
(before I understood)
The complexity of our love
How time
distance
and humor
molded our peace

Lunchtime in downtown L.A.
Our little Thai spot on Sunset
one of the few times
you saw me
as me
(your "lil sis")

You said
you knew your life would end soon
You said...
...I wrote
Didn't want to make it past forty
And yet
Something, someone
came along and everything changed
And you almost made it
to 45

I wonder...
Is this how you saw it play out?
The tragic ending to the immigrant underdog story?
The coming of age for many a melanated man
whose wings expanded far and wide
shadowing the doubt
and despair
soaring beyond
                        anyone's reach
Only
to watch yourself
burn

Memories of you
lost to time
and severed ties
Secrets and dreams
buried with you
Across the world
Down in the global South
a country whose earth I've never touched
Yet so close
to the land
you once
called home
Your body waiting
to return...

So much was left unsaid
The bruises and scars
of our tangled history

Written across my skin,
the sweltering shame
that envelops my body
sinking my heart deep
into the pit
of my bowels

The fear rising

I
have
so much
to say

"The truth is...."

      I swallow it whole
until I can't hold it down much longer
The wicked truth
of your demise
The sickness that strikes
My body
regurgitating our reality
Spewing Its vitriol
through every orifice and pore

My fear suppressing my freedom
Containing its toxicity
Maintaining appearances

Joey
Paquito
José

the asshole who hit and hurt
with words and fists
fed me lies and
          late night Mickey-D's
to make up for
the bruises and insecurities
he bequeathed me
even in death

You
        Are
King

Bigger than life
keeper of secrets and tales
I will never hear

May the world tremble
at the outrage
of our tightly-sealed lips
Retaining the fabricated
Fairytale ending
You did not deserve
May the truth resurface
in a fiery blaze
destroying everything
in its path
Consuming those of us
who had no choice
but to feel the truth of your loss
May your freedom come
When we speak your truth
When we take your body
Out of foreign land
And return you home

Joey
Paquito
José

Act of Contrition

I sacrifice my painstaking attempts of fitting into
single-digit sized jeans and pretty/thin privilege,
counting calories and dress sizes down to nothing.
I purge my sins, gripping porcelain with white-knuckled fear.

"You look so great! Whatever you're doing, keep doing it."

My body, the measure of all my worth
and the less of *it* there is,
the more of me is *yours* to consume.
But I wonder, when will it finally be *mine?*

Human Sacrifice

El mango,
ripe with juice
dripping down my right hand.
Overindulging in the fullness of your entirety.
Sunshine-yellow flesh viciously torn between my teeth,
sticking tiny tendrils of fruit to my underfed lips.
I devour you with the determination of a starving animal
ravaging the hunted prey it's been violently denied.
My fist clenched tight around its seed
like a deathgrip to the heart. Bloody and torn,
squeezing shame and guilt through my slippery fingers.
Its fuzzy edges digging through my sticky palm,
smearing the fortune on my hand into near nothingness.
I am a child gorging on sweets overcome with regret,
sick and satisfied by the flood of its golden nectar.
My face stained in pulp, spit and tears like a lioness post-hunt.
               Was it worth it?
The need for love and attention only American beauty can bring.
Nobody told me the price would be so high.

Memory Game

My friends tell me, it can't always be about race,
The neglect from doctors, teachers, and grownups
tell me I'm wrong
that I am broken
as though the skin that covers my every inch can't be seen
or unseen by wandering eyes

It can

But then I remember the little Salvadorean bakery 10 minutes from my house
With the MAGA wearing white man who fixes the ovens and comes in and out of the back door like he owns the place
        he doesn't
He can't!
I hold my breath and pray he doesn't see me
my eyes are closed and the sudden chill overcomes me like

That time in Lake Tahoe when we gathered around
jugando Lotería after a delectable dinner
the snow slowly falling outside and the warmth of the fire bringing us closer, calmer
You can't be Salvadoran, you're American, it's like me saying I'm Irish
I laugh and I sigh because, *guess what* I told him

I can

Requiem For A Relationship

She's out there somewhere
a name buried in the depths of my mind
with a vague memory of a gentle face
much like mine at the time
but without the bitterness of rejection
permanently affixed

Thirty years have passed
since we last crossed paths
and still
I wonder if she remembers
that day, that moment
the brief encounter that's haunted me
since before we met
before I even knew...

I think about you
wherever you are
and I wonder
what amazing things
we could have done
together
had we been raised
          under the same roof or
even traded weekends
at our mama's houses

To play.
To love.
To grow.
Together.

I don't know you but I want to know you
The highs and lows that make up the story of your journey
The flames that forged you into the cachimbona you are today
How the history of our ancestors flows through your veins
and pushes you towards your higher self...
                        how it does with me.
Silence and fear overcome me
A scorching wave of shame
that billows wildly
from my skin into my soul
where I retreat in its
infernal discomfort

I want to know you,
dear sister...
and yet I fear
it's not what's meant to be

She's out there, somewhere...
a name buried in the depths of my mind
yearning and fighting to be heard,
to be said...
        to reclaim
the connection that's long been denied

What great things
could we have done
dear sister
had we never been torn apart?

Men

My biggest weakness is appealing to your humanity,
treating you the only way I know to treat others —
often better than I treat myself.
I will go hungry for you,
lose sleep over you.
I hold back tears and words and feelings
for you and your comfort.
It hurts me
when I try to show you even a little bit,
how quickly you admonish my heart.
Somehow I'm still paying for the sins of my father.

Anhelo

Los días son largos sin ti,
pero cada momento se corta
al recordar que no estás aquí.

From Lust We Have Loved and Lost

In the kitchen of my 526 sq.ft. apartment
late one night,
you knocked on my door.

Silver flask in hand,
those sky-blue eyes glazed over
with bourbon-kissed lips
drenched in shame and
the lingering scent of penitence
seeping through.

The burgundy empress skirt I wrapped
high around my waist that morning,
riding high above my legs over my sacrum
and that one tattoo that only you and a few have seen.
Your hands holdfast onto my core,
my heart beating trepidatiously.
All I want is more.

I grip the edge of the counter.
The scent of whiskey whispering in my ear,
"This is real".
As you pushed your unapologetic regret
into my soft, brokenhearted body.
Crushed by the weight of your lies and disrespect,
and whatever it was *we* were.

Whatever we were,
you said
"we had good times",
but it didn't matter.

I didn't matter,
except in that dark moment.
Our bare feet pressed firm upon the cold indigo tile,
and for once, I felt yours.

You came clean onto my floor.
My tears and your guilt manifesting
a milky malaise, glistening by the fading footprints.
Tracking your departure out of my life and out my door,
imprinting the moment you showed me
what real love meant to you, and what I abhor.

The ghost of our failed friendship
disappearing with you into the darkest of nights
until I let you hurt me once more.

The Housecleaner's Daughter

Is it strange that I still think of you?
Playing in your backyard,
where the grass was always much greener, lusciously grown, and manicured
An entire world left outside the verdant canopy of your lot
What would I say to you if I had the chance?

I'm sorry I read your diary when you weren't home
I kept your secrets to myself, some of them were so much like my own

For playing with your Super Nintendo
while you and your family were away
Instead of dusting and tidying el desorden of your den
For all the string cheese and handisnacks
you never got to eat after school
                        they were the meals I needed to get through
The long workday mama dragged me to
My dirty chuck taylors with the rainbow laces
Kept under the writing desk in your kitchen
The scent of pine sol diffusing the air
soaking the wood floors
My way of letting you know that you were safe
that we were one/the same

I wanted you to see me like I saw you

We were children
from two worlds apart
I a stranger in your home
a place I'd learn to know so well
it haunts my dreams until this day
The emptiness
The luxury
The fear

My existence
An imposition
A stain on the image of
Your perfect smile
and heavenly blue eyes
Windexed clean
As though I was never there

Demasiado Is a Bad Word

I grew up believing,
feeling,
thinking
demasiado is a bad word.

Come demasiado.
Habla demasiado.
Está demasiado gorda,
demasiado negra.

Y en turno trate de no ser demasiado nada.
Calladita,
palidita,
flaquita.
Pero nunca pude ser *demasiado* de esas cosas,
No matter how hard I tried.

Heatstroke

You were not the first body to fall before me,
flirting with death and the heart on my sleeve.
To see you lifeless on the floor,
holding your body up and feeling
all of your weight upon my arms as I beg you to
please wake up.
Your eyes wide-open, pupils dilated.
Speechless and stiff,
you looked just like she did, helpless and cold.
This isn't your time; it's too soon.
Please wake up.
I can't lose you too.

Notes from a 10 AM Appointment

In which our protagonist enters the zoom room for a psych evaluation
Eager and nervous to uncover the next phase of her healing journey.

The 'doctor' tells her

That's a lot of loss for someone to have experienced by your age

Borderline Personality disorder...
but it has nothing to do with your personality...

You've experienced significant trauma...

Care provider burnout...

...you were too young...

      It's impacted your development...

      You must feel like you were robbed of your childhood...

      It's clear you have a complicated post-traumatic stress disorder...

      Today it could be BPD, tomorrow it could be ADHD...

At the center of it all is your trauma.

He asks her where her family is from, she tells him El Salvador...

I'm sure that must've come with its own set of challenges

She smiles
the words "epi-ge-ne-tic trau-ma"
climb up her spine
Each letter
expanding
      into the spaces
between   her   vertebrae
Urging her to shout
their collective
      string
      of
      truth
Instead
she smiles
and says nothing

Ad Nauseam

Chronic illness rears its ugly head
today is not a normal day
it never is
the pain accumulates
in the pits of my stomach
       the familiar pain that's followed me since childhood
Dolores, my friend
discomfort incarnate

when rest is not enough
the comfort foods of yesteryear no longer soothe
the rampant chaos churning in my core
I grow stagnant
incapable of feeling
anything but
the shame
the fear
       of help
no,
asking for help
no,
being vulnerable
no,
being rejected
no,
being insignificant
yes

all of the above
sometimes there is no relief
sometimes it lingers for hours
days
weeks
it feels like a lifetime

it's been a lifetime

A Few Things About Regret

Regret is the bitter aftertaste
that lingers after swallowing your pride
It's saying the things that need
to be said to people you love
The ones you know can do better
Be better and grow with you

Instead the gaping tension spans
more miles than the distance between
Leaving you with no choice but to retract
Because it's clear they never cared
the same way you do

Regret is the phantom feeling in your chest
that trembles at the silent shame of your youth
It's the hot flash that scorches you from
head to toe at the moment of hindsight

Like not being able to speak or comprehend
the colonizer language connecting you to
your elders and your roots
All while thinking that language is the only way
to communicate and express love

But the funny thing about regret is
after all of that heartache and time
You can look back and say
you know better now
and do your best
to have none

Veranera

She wades in the water
hands and arms stretched outward
spreading the soft foam of the waves
       to
       and from
              her body
the echo of her movements
captured by
the ripples in the
crystal-clear shore

Her flawless skin
       glowing
              under the summer sun
a gentle amber tone that
reveals her secret history
she wears proudly
with her heart on her sleeve
yet struggles to fully know
Understand

There is safety in these waters
something familiar
It overwhelms her senses
shakes her to her core
her tears
Rolling
   down
      her face
Indistinguishable
from the sea
that embraces her
delicate
   powerful
      being

this is supposed to be a happy place

There is longing in her soul
and in these waters
A calming relief
Refreshing her weary spirit
She smiles
Looking onto the horizon
Remembering
not too long ago
   mama looked out into
      the same golden skies
Basking in the
burning glory
of the very sun
kissing her skin
   the waves
washing away
her grief
   and rescuing
Her sinking
   heart

Try to Understand

My autistic brain
is not broken or wrong,
just wired differently than most ~~of the world's.~~
And in this neurotypical landscape,
I must blend in with the broad strokes
that paint the palatable picture you see before you.

The beauty is in the details,
the truth between the lines.
Shaping this multifaceted gem
shimmering bright,
blinding your eyes from the truth
that dwells beneath the diamond smile
and stoic facade.

My therapist says
I hide it well.
The mask comes on seamlessly
second nature and often
unbeknownst and automatically.
I've had years,
lifetimes,
to perfect who you want to see.
The person I've grown
to painfully believe
I need to be.

An entire lifetime,
past and present ripped away.
Hidden through history,
medical records, misdiagnoses,
extreme attempts to silence and suppress
the glory that I hold in this mind of mine.

This world is determined to
silence my voice,
grind my bones into the ground,
forcefully fit me into boxes of mediocracy and meritocracy.
My body and mind an act of resistance
from the inside out.
Where the ashes will rise and fill the air,
calcifying the essence of my spoken word
in the tender lining of your lungs.
My words speaking through your tired breath,
realizing themselves into crystalline shards
of poetic truth and the justice that only my words can bring me.
Poetry is the only time I can show you
the truth of who I am.
It's in the nuances,
the repetition,
reflection,
repetition,
nuances.
The truth of who I am?
Poetry is the only time I can show you.

Birth of a Poet

I've been making moves
since before I was born
long before I could put
words to sounds
and thoughts on paper
Crossing boundaries
              borders
                          and people
Straight outta the womb
Head first and fisticuffed
Fighting to be heard
and begging to be seen
Dug myself into
an early grave
Rising above
the impossible
Reclaiming
the stolen bounty
of my self-worth

Watch me flourish
and grow up
An age
I never thought possible
Learning and loving
with patience and
understanding que
Nací media muerta
Como la gente de mi tierra
Después de la noche roja del '32
Una noche inolvidable y ignorado
La sangre de Feliciano y
nuestros antepasados
            desconocidos
La lengua de nuestro ancianos
            Rompida
                    Mudos
a la realidad de nuestra historia
de nuestra tierra Negra
A history of violence
coursing through my veins
its torrid memories
burning in my blood

Raised in a lineage
of warriors incarnate
fit for a modern world war
Biding my time
Armed
with centuries
of rage
            honor
                        and a silver tongue
Ready to unleash and release
An onslaught of truth
Transcribing
ancestral pain
From deep within the
                    Darkest
            depths
of my heart

Rising up
from the bottom
Now I'm here
Gritando con ganas
La historia de mi gente
Pérdida al tiempo
Y la ignorancia
Recién encontrado
en mis sueños y
los suspiros
de mis antepasados
Desarrollando
Into *mi poder*
Where I stitch these rhymes
and post-colonial
collo-qui-a-lisms
Spitting them
loud and proud
Setting us

    And we

        And me

            Free

With no
rhyme or reason
But simply

To be

CHAPTER 2
The Light

Canción del Colibrí

Sigue el sol entre las nubes
y detrás de las montañas.

Calladita en la calma de la mañana,
donde nadie te oiga y no te distraigas.
Quédate pendiente de mis mensajes.

En las canciones de las alondras
                              y los zancudos,
el colibrí y los ronrones
volando libre en tu presencia.

Báñate en el calor del amanecer,
y deja que la luz de mi amor
derrita tus penas en su brillo.

A Prayer For The Most Imperfect Love

There is a myth about love
that it is a choice
That we move about our day
relationship to relationship
choosing who we let in
                              And out
Love is beyond a battlefield
it is the war that I have
with myself
The fight to reach the mirror
and see me
with lovelorn eyes of
one who has been rejected
one who was never enough
(Or simply, just too much)
An exaggeration of emotion,
always **accentuating** and
emphasizing the frantic desire of being
enough

The story behind every scar
that held my deepest teenage secrets
the movements that remedy
the stagnant energy
that consumes me
on the heaviest of days
I've battled with demons
who feed on my fears
hurling false advertisements
of promises
            unfulfilled
My body morphing
into the many shapes
and sizes
this world wants me
to fit into
but only for so long
because this skin

with its wrinkles,
        lonjas and scars
Is sacred

It is a vessel
that travels between
an ancient plane
to tell you, us
that love is
our divine right

Your body
a temple
worthy of the offerings
soaring
in the winds
that carry us through

Know that you are
divine and immaculate
In your existence
Carry that message
into the future
and remember

that this moment,
right now
is what we have left
and in this moment
surrender yourself
        to the unrequited love
Your body holds
for you
Because yes
Love is a choice
and your body
chooses you
every timet

Mañanas En El Jardín

Desde mi jardín miro el mundo pasando
Los aviones llenos de sueños y vacaciones
Pajaritos cantando su bella canción
Con la Sonora Dinamita prendido en el aire
Una mañana llena de reflejos y recuerdos
De un tiempo cuando bailábamos juntas
Bajo del sol en tu querido Sonsonate
Y la luna en la calle 29
Madre colibrí saludando me con sus pío píos
Flotando en frente de mis ojos
Cargando un mensaje de Dios y los angelitos
Tan cerca que te puedo abrazar
Pero mas lejos que puedo alcanzar
Desde mi jardín encuentro tus besitos del ayer
En la naturaleza espiritual
Y el calor de tu amor
En el sol alumbrando mi día

Heatwave

It's hot
82 degrees at 945pm
Record-breaking
Beaming

Hot

Skin glistening
Sticking slipping sweating
Sliding slowly
as you move
Pooling collecting coating the
back of the knees
that tender fold
You secretly touch
to feel its
damp dewy desire

Mosquitos tryin it
Slippin thru
sucking the sweetness outta you
Swatting squishing swaying away
Airplanes flying overhead
Birds only dream of reaching such heights
My caged heart sings the same tune
Like a broken record
Skipping to the end
Seeking sweet
Relief

Ode To Chronic Illness

When the music hits it feels so good
Pero esas cumbias hit different
All over my body
the same way
the pain
rides through my nervous system
Infecting every bit of me   that moves
with every breath
every step
and the blink of my   eyes
Jumping across the pain scale
4 to 10 in less than 5   on a good day a solid 7 and
                    You just grin AND BEAR IT

It used to be you had to hide
the feelings that infect you deep inside
Clench your teeth
(to the gritty grinding of the beat)
Jaw gets tighter
                    (extracting the high pitched twinging in your ears)
melodically balanced
with the gentle bravado
of your ex-halation
                    An ex-altation to the pain
grooving to the sweet sounds
of the orchestra
A cacophony of oppression
Reverberating from my soul
My body a conduit between
this new age suffering
And our historic struggle
Manifesting into this silent battle
                    that I fight

Migraine to migraine
Backache to backache
Every sleepless night
Music is my liberation
The medicine to my soul

The bridge between two realms in which
I coexist
Longing to return
to the bittersweet nest
Where the music echos into the waves
and travels oceans far and wide
Just to find me again

To El Salvador, With Love

Mi pulgarcito
mighty and divine
A tiny imprint
nestled in the luscious landscape
of primeval splendor
Breaking through the thicket
of despair and destruction
Erupting
through the blood-soaked earth
permeating the air
with our forgotten stories, our songs

Reclaiming your joyful existence
through our daily resistance
Surviving the oncoming and
ever-present storm
Greying and hiding
your horizons
Forever beyond our reach

You are
the greatness that has flourished
and overgrown
into a bounty of precious fruits;
plump with the bitterness of grief
the viciously viscous sweetness
of resilience
clinging to our parched mouths
The juicy truth
      dripping
            down
                  our
                        lips
with every word
We utter
      Every sip
            We swallow

El lindo sol
calentándote tu carita
blessing you with the love and grace
of its infinite strength
An immovable force
that bellows
with every voracious
Eruption
Past and present
Anointed in the heavenly waters
of your shores
Your legacy of triumph
over unspeakable injustice
The warriors of
a people surviving
war and globalization
The children of diaspora
free to live the life
         we are owed
Free to live
the life we deserve
To one day return to you
Mi querido pulgarcito
Mighty and divine

Las Flores

Dos flores del mismo jardín
La luna y el sol
Juntas al fin
después de tanto tiempo

Regando el calor de nuestra piel con la manguera
Como nuestros días en el barrio
Antes que piscinas y oportunidades entraron a nuestra vida

Una juventud llena de dolor y alegría
La miramos de enfrente
Dejando las penas atrás en nuestra vista
Mientras seguimos viviendo
Con gozo poderoso
Creciendo

Colectando nuevos momentos
De nuestra nueva juventud
Disfrutando el presente
Cosechando la abundancia
Que nuestra madre sembró
Cuando cruzo la frontera

Nochebuena (A Very 29th Street Christmas)

Navidad en nuestra casa was a sacred melange of cultures,
a clash of tribute and traditions melding together
for a vibrant evening of celebración y emoción.

We celebrate on Christmas Eve.
The crescendo of festivities harmonizing with
the old school cumbias of America Central,
and as the day progressed, so did the volume.

Las cumbias begin as early as the sunrise,
welcoming the boisterous energy of our songs.
Mami always keen to keep us moving,
keep us joyful. 'Tis the season, after all.

She cooks and cleans all night.
It's what she does, and
oh my, does she do it well.

Her hips swaying to the Banda Blanca beat
as she glides across the kitchen floor,
reveling in the warmth of that old-school music heat.

Her mop in hand trapeando fast,
su piso brillando el camino where hearts and hunger meet
laughter, songs, and happy feet.

Navidad pa nosotros means
pan con chumpe jugosito y delicioso,
tamales al gusto wrapped in banana leaf,
served con pan francés or Weber's white bread.
Tía's strong arm stirring the masa con ganas,
never missing a beat from the music blasting through.
Adding sazón de cada rincón, that spice of life mingling and simmering
with the scent of mami's masa mixing and marinating.

Mami was no stranger to hunger.
A whole year's worth of savings dressed and plated,
wrapped and tagged.
Always enough food to go around.
"Aquí nadie muere de hambre," she would say.
Never one to turn a hungry stranger away.

The DJ's blasting jams out the driveway.
Strobe light flashing bright,
pickup trucks and hoopties rattling,
bumping with the glorious Garífuna beat
Todo mundo sabe que la parranda nunca para en nuestra casa.
Todo mundo cantando no matter lo que pasa.

We know all the words but don't really know what they mean.
Our laughter and joy perfuming the air with all of our being
as we get together and sing the classic "Jingle Bells" ring,
those merry songs we dance and sing.
La cumbia sampuesana, la que bailan con ganas.
Y claro también the one we can jam all day,
Sopa de Caracol. (EY!)

Presents at midnight,
sleepy little brown eyes keen to see what's inside
the gently wrapped gifts hiding under the noble fir.

Their tiny eager hands are waiting to tear through,
and the grown-ups are just getting started too.
Our music and life still filling the air as the evening dims
and the little ones drift into dreams.

The cops would shut us down, but on 29th Street
Mama is king and what she says goes.
It helped that she'd offer up a plate and a smile,
coqueteando her way into a warning and an evening
worthy of the title *Noche Buena*.

We never spoke of Navidad in the motherland,
but this was what we had, and it was then as it is now.
The memories of home that mami passed down,
the music and food of our people that survived,
all that was left when she left it all behind.
Christmas in our home away from home.
We play the same songs even now,
inviting and honoring those beyond
as she did then,
so we do now,
cada Nochebuena

Regalitos

Jugo de manzana,
té de manzanilla.
Estas son los cosas
con que mi mami me cuida.

Besitos en la frente,
cosquillas en la espalda,
sus deditos caminando,
"Carnita, carnita,"
cosquilleando mi brazo.
Sacándome las risas y las lágrimas,
la magia de sus manos limpiando,
bendiciendo mi alma y ser.

Uñitas filadas rascándome la corona,
desenredando nudos y mis penas.
El sonido de sus pequeño movimientos
Como canciones de amor eterno.
Entregando el cariño divino
que solo una madre puede regalar.

Tela

Tengo una foto de ti
Dormida en la playa encima de
una toalla
Chunky Valentino sunglasses
covering half your face
Toda mechuda
y en tu lime-green bikini
La tela
puesta como una falda
Faranduleando
como siempre y
sin querer

Esa tela
es una de las pocas cosas
que me quedan
de ti

Mi tela divina
Protegiendome con
amor, estilo y sabiduría
The sacred tapestry on the
divine playground
of my ofrenda
Donde tu espíritu
se pone a chismear con
los ancestros y
A cantar con los angelitos
San Judas
holding haters
at bay

Where
fervent prayers
and dutiful offerings
deliver us from
loneliness and despair
Dust, ash and wax drippings
Conchas, fotos y recuerdos
Adorning your
hallowed cloth
Tu tela bendita
an extension of you
The devotion
to tradition.
The cloth.

The connection.
The fabric of time
in life and beyond
The unbreakable bond
Woven together by your
love and care
Pulling me closer
Closer
To my higher self
It is her.
It is home
It is
Always

Lucero

Red and vibrant
shining through
the infinite darkness

Brighter than
the Sun that
beckons life

Heart of the scorpion
it's no coincidence
she rests within your light

Your duplicitous nature
revealing your truth
Aligning and
teasing the skies

A celestial celebration
Spanning beyond time
and the blackness
between the stars
La parranda infinita
Anti-Ares
No room for war
internal or external
Show thyself as you are
Autenticaaaa

Armed at the ready
Super(fly) giant
Slick and sly

Let me mimic
that war cry
Lemme radiate
your prodigious power
Far beyond
my tiny human reach
These stiff
achy fingers
creaky knees
patojiando o no
will keep on
shining on
Porque
ser humano
si se puede
y se pudo

Bajo la guía
de tu brillo
Y el poder
de los antepasados
descansando
in your scarlet surrender

Gold teeth shining
bright up the skies
Illuminate

This expansive path
Unfurling
becoming
darkness eternal

Spanning lifetimes
and light years
growing brighter
until it's gone

Thirst Trap #1

I am a child of the fucking sun
Revived by its light
Warmed by its delicious radiance
My skin absorbing
its life-giving rays
A beacon of hope
Glowing majestically
Upon the landscape of
this expansive body
its rolling hills
and tender mounds
For you to revel
in the glory of
my fatness
a delicious invitation
For you to explore
Trace with your peering eyes
Curious for what's beneath the glow
The mysteries hidden in the folds of my skin
Your silence broken by my consenting smile
Loud enough to bring you to your knees
Surrendering, seducing, softly
Take this light and make it yours
Make it shine
Lips glistening
Thirst quenched
Breath taken away
Spellbound by
the warmth of my body
Ready for more

Undercover

Bring me the warmth of your embrace.
Legs wrapped and lost beneath these tangled sheets,
the softness of your touch upon my scarred skin awakens my fragile
heart.
Forgiveness blooms with every tender kiss you plant upon my being.
The heat of your hands melting through the tension, softening my hold,
easing my worries and woes deep beneath the rest of me, releasing our
forbidden shame.
A prediction of what's to come when curious hands and hungry hearts
come together.

Madrugadas

Despierto
al sonido de
tus sueños
y los gritos
de mi espalda
Un dolor fuerte
como los truenos
de las noches
más oscuras y pesadas

Los movimientos
de tu cuerpo sobre el mío
agitando mis sentidos
Mis ojeras
reteniendo
los secretos del ayer
y las pesadillas
de mi realidad

La noche
se derrite entre el día
La luna
callándose
en la oscuridad
coqueteando
El sol
sube sobre los árboles
Su brío
blanqueando
mi vista

La silueta
de las montañas
pintando el cielo
con su gran ser
achicándome
en su lucero
La luz
del amanecer
me deslumbra
Las bullas de la vida
listas pa entrar
a un nuevo paso
Me mueve
abierta para las nuevas
posibilidades
de un nuevo día

Dance Like No One Is Watching

But
you still
hold back
because you feel
like **they are,**
and that's
the **anxiety**
creeping up.
But at least
Beyoncé was playing,
and you could **just**
release it all
in song and **dance**
to the beat
in full blast
because **nobody**
is home
and you can just
let loose,
and **this is it.**
this I[s] what
freedom feels like,
typos and all.

Big Mouth

I believe that everything I say is poetry.
How can anything that comes in and out of this mouth be anything less?

Recarga las Pilas

Beh!
Ya ni te reconozco.
Tus ojos cansados de no dormir,
la rapidez de tu mente que no te deja tranquila.
Pura ansiedad.

Muévete más despacio.
Lenta pero segura. Mientras sigas tu camino un día llegaras.
Descansa
y en la madrugada cuando los suspiros de tu aliento escapan de tu ser,
recuerda que la magia de la vida se encuentra
dentro nuestras palabras y el silencio que dejamos florecer.

The Most Vibrant You

Slow down and slip into
This great unknown
The binaries of life left outside
The colors of every feeling
Emerging from your darkness
illuminating
a glorious spectrum
of love and
endless possibilities

Emanating from your heart

A rose gold glow
Breaking through the bullshit
Warming that bitter blue heart
Billowing away those ghastly grey
nimbus clouds obscuring your view
Silver lining passing thru
Painting sadness bright with
Glorious green, optimist orange
bad bitch brown
and radical rouge

Blooming a new breed
of abstract artistry
Familiar but oh so fresh
Paint and rain spilling over
Mixing a mess of genuine joy
And humble hues gathered
From the goodness and gold
That Rests within you

You make it so hard to love you, and yet I can't help but to choose you every time- **Bad Habit**

Eye of the Beholder

Staring at this body in the mirror,
its folds and flaws building you up.
You tear yourself down.

This world for so long taught you to see
how you were not the ideal.
Undesired and never enough.

And with time you will realize,
through blood, sweat, and tears,
the truth behind all that they'd scrutinize.

You are the beauty of life and divine,
the voice and the cries breaking
through the glass ceiling,
looking down upon the beauty
you have always been.

Build yourself up and look into your eyes.
Tell yourself to break through all the lies
and learn to love the you that has always been.

A reflection of glory in this beautiful skin you're in.

Las Comadres

Ellas que siempre están ahí,
de lejos y cerca,
pendiente de las penas,
consumiéndote de adentro.

Las cheras del ayer,
con las que te pasabas al libre.
Ellas que dejaron sus marcas en tu memoria.

Los chistes y chismes que te recuerdas en los momentos sin luz.
Las risas y el calor de nuestra conexión al recordar que
nunca estás sola querida amiga.

Las comadres siempre se quedan de pie.
Las de los corazones enormes y brazos fuertes.
Ellas que comparten palabras y la magia de su poder.
Esas mujeres que siempre te quieren ver triunfar,
llegar más lejos que nosotros podemos imaginar.

Ellas que respiran amor y platican verdad.
Agridulce como las mejores bebidas de aquellas noches.
Algunas que recordamos, y otras que quisiéramos olvidar.
Esas ahí son tu ride or die.
The homies who stayed,
saw you for you.

Pura auténticas y dispuestas a lo que sea porque
las comadres son las que siempre están ahí.
Son las chingonas que cruzan y quiebran fronteras.
Ellas que te dan sus manos cuando necesitas alguien que te recoja.
Ellas que te mandan a la mierda cuando te sale la perra de adentro.
Ellas que siempre abren sus brazos y corazones,
listas para recibir tu amistad y tu paja porque ellas son
más que familia, más que amiga y mentor.
Ellas son tus comadres y como ellas no hay mejor.

Manos de Gracia

Pupusas hechas a mano
No hay ninguna otra manera
Entre los dedos y tus palmas
Creamos una memoria deliciosa
Las manos y maneras de
nuestras madres de ayer

Tortillando la masa
Con paciencia y prisa
Pasando nuestra historias secretas
Con gusto y sazón
De nuestra tierra querida
Hoy y para siempre

El calor del comal dispara
Un aliento en el aire
Queso quemadito con la mezcla de manteca
Los sentidos revueltos en todo mi ser
Cocinado así es un arte divino
Perdido al tiempo

Que suerte
Saborear el amor
De tus manos y corazón
Aqui en mi cocina

Fuck the Fork

We eat with our hands
a natural connection to the earth
honoring las manos
that cultivated the grains
ground the masa
and shaped the tortillas
Generously serving a meal
fit to devour
with one's own skin

Our hands
that touch the food
we've shared
laughed
and grieved into
Kneading the memories
of our past
into the daily bread
that feeds us
the truth of our divinity
that lives and grows into the soil
Lingering in the air we breathe
expanding up and outward into the heavens
A humble reminder
That we partake only to return
to that
from which we came
Bellies full of love
and lavish
abundancia

Our hands
the vessel to deliver and receive
the bounty worthy of our
insatiable desire
to remember
That we are one

Ancestral Reminders

I am back with my ancestors when
I feel the breeze across my face
Their gentle whispers
singing through
the birds chirping
their whistles
keeping the beat

To the song of my people
that plays in my heart

                The beat
                to my own drum
                that I dance to
                when no one is watching

The pitter patter of
my heart racing
with a tempo of temptation
playing in my head

I'm back with my ancestors
when we're blasting those cumbias
in glorious praise of the life we've been given
The blessing of our pasts
Connecting my soul
to the roots of my history
to the branches of my present

Reaching high and wide
harvesting strange fruit
Bearing bitterness and brawn
Flourishing in the flowers
of our future

I am with my ancestors
when they hold me
in their power and proclaim
that they are always with me
and they have never left

Tengo un chingo de mamis que me han dado más de lo que puedo dar
que suerte tener tanto amor en tan poco tiempo
-Mujeres Divinas

Delightful Duplicity

I revel in the truth of the present
> *Knowing that this is only the beginning*
The future a distant vision beyond
> *Reach forward and surpass your earthly grasp*
Holdfast to the truths that come from
> *Healing the difficult past that follows us*
Within your heart is the story of
> *Pain and joy unparalleled ready to release*
Your spirit, surviving and soaring
> *The best is yet to come*

Sleepless in Seattle

You can't catch up on sleep.
There's not enough time,
and yet there is nothing but
a ringing in my ears.
A symptom of age and distress.
Tracing the lines of your face in front of the mirror,
noticing the wrinkles on your hands. Wondering,
have they always been this way?
I'd say they look like mama's but
her thumb was short and wide,
the opposite of mine.

Do you see her story in your eyes?
In the creases of your skin, where your smile lines
reveal the joys of a past long forgotten.

Shifting the focus away from the grief and into
the warmth of my bed, where I patiently lay.
Tossing and turning to the ticking of the clock,
resting to the trembling hum of the 3 a.m. flight path overhead.

I pray for relief within this healing cloud of restitution.
The ringing growing dimmer as the lights lay low,
the weight of my eyelids dropping heavily.
My breath becoming deeper as my body sinks into itself,
slipping quietly into whatever is left of the night.

Siempre Stoned

Me llaman la marijuanera,
siempre stoned y con flojera.
Bicha malcriada sin vergüenza,
pero a mi me vale verga.

Me llaman maldita marijuanera,
con hojas y flores de donde quiera.
Humo de gratitud disipando
con mis ancestros libre en el aire flotando.
Llena de gracia y yerba buena,
llevándote a lo más alto que yo pueda.

Me siento mejor cuando fumo.
Inhalando la riqueza del mundo,
exhalando las penas y mentiras
que respiro día tras día.

Aquí hay solo buena vibra.
Deja tus preocupaciones afuera
y bienvenida a la buena vida.

The magic of life is found in our words and the silence between them
- Shhh!

Poetic Infinita

What is poetry
but the voice for the voiceless
The language of
the unheard written across
time and space
The mother tongue
of many unrolling universal truths
The inside/out for all to see
The echoes of joy and surrender
raw and authentic

A hidden gem
buried in the ruins of despair
You can be anyone
You can be no one
Have it all or lose it all
Rebuild reframe and reconsider
the world as we know it

It is hope contained
Released upon hungry eyes
curious ears
tempered tongues
and hurried hands
Ready
to embrace
the majestic movement
these words
can bring

Poetry
like water
bread
and love
is for everyone
the silver lining cutting through
the darkness that envelops the skies
a break in the downpour
offering shelter
and light

The refuge we seek
when grasping for safety
Taking our breath away and
breathing life into our tired hearts
It's the darkness and the light
an offering suited
for each suffering soul
absorbing its power

It's the music
that sings us to sleep
quiets our minds

breaks us open
and amplifies
our cries

The beauty
in our mistakes
the lessons learned and
the rewards we reap
retelling their richness

They are the rise
and fall
of our dreams
and reality
The healing that happens
when no one is looking

When all eyes are on you
and no one can hear you scream
it is the space between the stars
and the infinite glow
the land that's been taken
and the reclamation of
spirit and song

Poetry is a spell
cast upon our hearts
bewitched with
larger than life glory
An affirmation
or hidden message
ready to be revealed
the magic never ending
getting stronger
with every
word

It is the escape
from danger
a place of understanding
connection and hope
meeting us with

shock awe and joy
always where we are
and always when
we need it most
if we only know
where to look

What is poetry
but the life we wish to see
for each other
An open invitation to receive
an endless expanse
of eternal emotions
unleashing the truth
of our humanity
and our hearts

CHAPTER 3

The Storm

MotherTongue

I do not speak the language of my people
it was taken from me
like the land I so lovingly speak of
I do not know my history
as far as my abuelita y su nana
the pillars of my creation
indebted to the creator
filling me with truth and feelings
that were once lost to time
crushed by the American dream
when all I ever dream of is
this place called home
that I don't even know but
only in dreams does it feel real

Wake Up

The colonizers got me all fucked up
thinking I wouldn't come
for what is mine
is ours
The bounty of liberation
lost to war   algorithms   and time
It's running out
but you see
Most people run from their mistakes
I run to them
with open arms
Listening listlessly
learning the longest lesson earned and
replenishing my power
with rest and sweet
dreams of retribution
Whispered by my ancestors
their tender smiles and powerful praise
pushing me forward
with a vengeance
Sparking the fire
within my soul
Igniting the fury
in my subconscious
The slumbering beast who knows
the recurring ill-will imparted upon it
Feeling the sting of the lashes
and the burn of the bullets
Piercing through my consciousness
Awakening   to the   cold sweats
purifying my body from
the historical fallacies
Fabricating my reality
In this already artificial world
Rising up and
out and into
My new self

Father Sky Said To Me

"Forgiveness don't come easy.
*   See, you and I are cut from the same cloth.*

Heir to miracles and visions beyond her understanding.
Heal those wounds,
*   let me lick them clean.*

Vast with endless combinations of beauty
and infinite possibilities of natural reflection.
Made in the image of divine perfection."

Rivers and oceans of tears, dried and barren.
Parched and dusty is my mouth until
rain falls upon my eyes and I see clearly.

Father Sky quells my cries quenching the thirst
born from the drought and dispossession from the divine
He reminds me I was never alone under his infinite embrace
All i have to do is look up and open my eyes to the possibilities
Dwelling in the din of darkness and resting in the power resting of light
Father Sky wipes the slate of sorrow clean and whispers in my hopeful
ears *"the rain has come and you **will** rise anew"*

Battle-Ready

Take off your mask
and put on the armor.
Pieces of protection
acquired through time,
gathered graciously.
Gifted generously
by those who came before
and held me tenderly.

The women whose shoes
always felt too big to fit into.
The many miles they traveled
to provide and power through.
Running,
        always running,
to make ends meet.

The strength of their arms
and the world they carry
on their shoulders.
Balancing entire
ecosystems,
        emotions,
and forces of nature
no man can contain.

My core encased
in their golden wings,
forged in the fires of fervent faith.
Taking that blind leap into believing
that this body is sacred
and worthy of safety.

The diamond in the rough shining bright,
fortified by the fury of their fight.
Sealed in their power with a hot-red kiss,
breathing fire through my crimson lips.

Spilling all the tea this blessed brown body
was forced to steep for too long.

My tender healing heart
beating bloody and bare
on the pedestal of self-sacrifice.
Armed and ready to take on the world
and take back what's mine.

So Where Do You Come From (No, Really!)?

A generational response to the age-old question most BIPOC get asked but with a bit more insight than usually given. The first verse is written from my mama's perspective, the second from my younger self and the third from where I am now

I

Yo soy (la hija de mi nana)
La hija de campesinos
fruteras and gamblers
Raised in the heart of
Sonsonate
Descended from
a people obliterated
through genocide
Caffeinated Corruption
       and U.S. imperialism on speed-dial
I fled with my two children
their cousins/my nieces
Left sisters, brothers
       and friends
far behind
beyond memory
and reconciliation
through long
blistered walks
crowded bus rides
evaded and embraced
checkpoints
along the way
(to the land of our Tongva brethren)
Away from air strikes
the charred stench
of singeing bodies
and diminished dreams
Here we are safe
Here we begin anew...

II

I am
the daughter of immigrants
Raised in the heart of South Central LA
West Side 'til I die
Deep in the 213 where
survival and rage
course through my veins
and into my heart
A rapacious desire
to reach far and beyond
whatever was left behind
Her story is not mine
my foolish disconnection
a blessing she bestows
yet fuels my existence
feeding the serpentine fulmination
that desires peace and security
the most basic of needs

There is silence

A broken language
lost to time
Communication
            and connection
Lost to the ages
We cannot speak of
the things we cannot name
The silence continues
for generations
Until…

III

I find my voice
through the trials
and traumas
of navigating
my inheritance
The fury

bestowed upon me
and mine
without consent or courtesy
for the humanity and heart
inside us all

I am
La Hija de Milagro
Daughter of miracles
To honor and uplift
        in these short verses
A journey through time
before
colonization
        and assimilation
Before
language
and lineage
hurled us into the void
away from history books
Chisme and chambre
I find myself here
through the gory/glory of resilience
It's pestilent revival
of a people long forgotten
by foreign minds
and pale gazes

I find myself here
to tell you
that my voice is not my own
It has traveled long and far
Body to body
Host to host
For centuries
before I could piece together
these ancient truths
you hear today

Forgotten and unknown,
some days just pass,
and I have nothing but
my words- Vacant

What the Mirones be Saying

When people tell me,
"You're so wise for your age!"
I say,
"That's the cost of growing up too early."

When people tell me,
"You're so resilient!"
I say,
"I have no choice; this is survival after all."

When people tell me,
"You're so exotic!"
I say
nothing and let my face do the talking.

When people tell me **anything** about my body,
I hold back the flooding memories of binging and purging from ages 4-34,
reinforced over time by people around me,
beyond me.

When people tell me,
"You make everything about race!"
I tell them,
*"That's because it is,
and if you can't see past your privilege,
then we done."*

Checklist

- ~~Take your medication~~
- ~~Drink water~~
- ~~Look out the window~~
- ~~Agonize over going outside~~
- Ahmaud was just running
- Somehow it!s 4pm and the sun is starting to set
- You!ve lost time again
- ~~Blast music as though no one is home~~
- the same playlist on repeat
- something familiar
- some kind of control
- You got this
- ~~Take your medication~~
- ~~Forget how to create~~
- mediocre poetry or some semblance of it
- forget how to write
- fall into a spiral of defeat
- Drink water
- Swim your way out
- Don!t forget to————-
- ~~(Wtf was that again?)~~
- ~~Rest and close your eyes~~
- Breonna was just sleeping

- In her own bed
- ~~Take your medication~~
- ~~Look both ways before you cross (anyone)~~
- Trayvon was just going home
- Stand your ground
- ~~Remember you are human~~
- Connected to kin
- Breathe in your grief
- George couldn!t breathe
- he was crying for his mama
- Remember you are healing
- You are not alone
- Breaking generational curses
- It's okay to cry for your mama
- ~~Remember to eat~~
- Despite the medication taking your hunger away
- Remember to forgive yourself
- When you forget any or all of the above
- ~~Remember to be gentle~~
- Because you!re still learning to love yourself
- Still learning to heal
- ~~Take your medication~~
- ~~Drink water~~
- ~~Try to fall asleep~~
- ~~Look out the window~~
- Breathe

Ravenous

The knot in my throat slides down slowly
undulating in the waves of stomach acid and pan dulce
a reminder that not everything goes down easy
            how does one prepare to grieve what has not yet been lost

I've lost so much already
mother, language, sister, brother
an entire nation of
campesions/guerrilleros
defending what is divinely ours
pillaged by
pale immigrant
invaders

Their ravenous desire
to consume/erase
Showing their true colors
Red WHITE and BLUE LIVES MATTER rhetoric
Some don't show any color
but the one of their skin and how
it stands out
       and above
the darker ones in the background
obscured by the radiant white smile this foreigner bears
His teeth betraying the supposed struggle
their privileged life knows nothing of

but hey they're "working on it" and I guess that's okay too

because we all have to start somewhere but
nevermind, y'all are 500 years late
to the early morning game
your wokeness only serving
the fragile ego
and socially distant
appraisal of your worth
       mine is less than
because you stand tall
and alone
while we stand back
wishing   waiting
for you to go back
from where you came from

The Audacity

A physiological response after Kamala Harris, the VP of the great American nation, uttered disrespect upon the Guatemalan people and all Central Americans looking for the same freedoms her hypocritical ass was afforded

"Don't come, do not come."
You are not wanted
Because give me your tired hungry and poor
does not apply to you
We do not want your children
your elderly and vi-rile
nor the stories they tell
the promises they keep
Do not come
For this land is not your land and to
"Proclaim LIBERTY Throughout all the Land unto all the Inhabitants Thereof"
Does not apply to you
who have raised cane corn and codices
long before this land knew the name

America
a nation we flee to
the illusion of safety
a land we die to call home
unbeknownst to us
weary travelers
seeking refuge from the rain
of terror cast upon us by
The ravenous monster
Devouring our culture
history and futures
this place where
we are unwanted
But desired

The truth is hard to swallow
Y El dicho
es sierto
not all skinfolk are kinfolk
And never forget
Que la boca come lo que le da las ganas

The Tale of The Melting Pot

I never liked the term "melting pot"because so much gets lost when blended and reduced. I have a hard time explaining why so, I hope this helps...

Once upon a time
We were told of the great melting pot
The bubbling cauldron where tradition and cultures
Brewed together a new mass
Selectively seasoning a palatable presence
Homogenized
like the land of milk and honey but
They never told us that the cream of the crop
that floats to the top
was the desired result
of the process

Pero like all delightful dairy
sitting and simmering
The taste begins to change
The curdled cries drowned by
the white lies
Begin to fester and froth
The narrative changing
Flowing outward/upward
reaching high above our eyes

An overflow of emotions
voraciously crashing upon the earth
moving entire mountains
yet gently wooing us
                    Our people
                    our land
to rest

Nosotros
La gente de agua maíz y café
We who steward our land
Cultivate our heritage

Our stories
Change the very terrain
that grounds us into
our higher purpose
Our spirits fortified
Amplifying our songs
Our cries-
          Can you hear it?
The rise of
our collective spirit
our healing...
the revolutionary renaissance
of a people long unheard
ready to cry out together that
we are here
and
we   are mighty
With the radiance of our melanated skin
The bounce of our hips
our powered-up fists
                    reaching for the sky
We soar
on the shoulders of our ancestors
Pouring out and over the melting pot
Overflowing back
onto that
which we've longed to know

Our selves
Our roots
Los sabores de nuestra tierra
Dulce como la miel
sin la amargura de leche ajena

Delicious liberation
clinging to our lips
Fingers dipped in desire
turning the page
to the next chapter
where we pass the torch
reminding our children
that

home is where the heart is
and we must shine
that light bright
to find our way back

From the perilously putrid pot
Breaking through
the hardened shell of shame
Holding us down

We lift us up
into the abundant gardens
that have nourished us since before
They built the table
that divides and conquers
This is reclamation
The rise and fall of the facade
that tips the scales
pouring the delicious truth
of our divinity
into the mouths of us
who hunger for revival
Feasting on the overdue
Freedom we've been denied

Sincerely, The Problem Woman of Color

June 16, 2021

To the white women at the PWIs
The ones who praised me
For being courageous
Heard my voice and passion
With fervor and approval, you who thought the
world of me, said you loved me, even claimed you
wouldn't let me go.
You forget I was a guest in your house/a
stranger to your customs and traditions; that in
fact I was not created equal and your policies
and procedures were not made for me (or with
people like me in mind).
When I told you this, through tears and fear,
agony and pain, you said I wasn't bringing my
all. Because you didn't see that all I had…you
took for granted.
You are the reason the cycle continues, the same
one we learned about sitting side by side
learning about DEI. You are the well-intended
white woman, the type you claimed you'd be
unlearning to become. The villain in the story
of another Black or Brown woman who was "too
much" when really, she was simply more than you
could ever handle.
Although a year has come and gone and the world
changed, our hearts transformed. I have yet to
see you show up the way you claimed you would,
for all the Black and Brown bodies that matter.
Because here I am, a whole year later still
waiting for the day you own up to the violence
you shed upon my existence; the betrayal of my
trust, rooted in your whiteness. Your silence
affirms that I DID NOT MATTER TO YOU AT ALL
Sincerely yours,

The Problem Woman of Color

PNW Wonderland

Driving down the Oregon coast
Traveling through sunset towns
afraid of being outside
(terrified) of being alone

I am a speck of darkness on the porcelain skin
of this great American town
An imperfection that is not welcomed
It's evident by the looks on their faces
The banners flying high
The stickers on their cars
Their maskless visages
with thin blue lines across their lips
My proximity to whiteness
my only salvation
My partner, my love
who does not fully see or grasp
the weight of this burden
I've carried across state lines
The grief of my ancestors
Inherited throughout generations
Navigating oppressive boundaries
A world that was rightfully ours
Mine
A world in which I'm seen as unworthy
A land where I am not safe
America, land of the free
Where dead men tell no tales
(their tongues cut off, their spirit silenced and blocked)
Where missing, murdered and indigenous women
have no future
But a past and present riddled with fear
and hope
For a better tomorrow
that perhaps
I and we
will never see

Block Battle

Karen from the block walks her dog without a leash.
Little Luna, soft and white, small, and presumably cute.
Cute enough, apparently, to walk her ever so freely.

Karen on the block gives Luna free reign.
Luna leads and scrambles, sometimes yapping
because that's what little dogs do.
Sometimes she calls her name,
"Luuuna."
Beckoning her closer, but Luna does not come.

Luna instead rushes freely toward me
and my little dog who is black, small, and unbiasedly cute.
Cute enough to keep on a leash, often a close one.

Little Luna charges and I freeze.

Karen from the block feels miles away.

My dog heels before I can find my words.

"Luna," she calls with very little concern or regard.

My dog already in my arms,
I try to walk away.
Luna follows.
I slide my foot forward,
the sound of my chancla
brushing the sidewalk
does nothing.

Karen from the block finally approaches,
sauntering *athleisurely* in our direction.
Hands occupied by diamonds and phone.
Quiet disregard across her tightly tied
ultra-high and mighty ponytailed face.

I am shaking,
I am afraid,
I am confused.

Because, really
what kind of person walks their dog without a leash
down a neighborhood street where children and
traumatized women of color live?
What level of entitlement enforces one to expect
everyone who crosses their path
to welcome their presence with praise when
all they can do is pray through the pain
and hope that this isn't the Karen that cries
her tears and repeats the ending we all know?

I swallow the fear.
Its burning shame sliding down my throat
reawakens my body.
Flushed and frightened,
the hot breath moving through my lips
whispering my words
despite the screaming inside.

"This isn't the first time your dog has done this to me."

I do not say anything else about
little leashless Luna.
I hold back my tears.

"She's really friendly," she says.

Karen from the block
is exasperated,
annoyed,
inconvenienced.

I wish I could say the same about
Karen from the block
that she said about little Luna.

I wish I could say that
this was the last time, but

Karen from the block insists on
unleashing little friendly Luna.

Unaware of the fear that builds
each time I go out the door,
The words that I practice in my head
over and over again, just in case
the breathing that becomes shorter,
faster.
The walks shorter,
faster.
Eyes moving,
looking, always
looking.

Because privilege and power move through these streets,
slithering deep into our ally's hearts and their fragile beats.
The virtue signals on their lawns ambivalently placed
right outside my home, where I'm supposed to feel safe.

The street where children play and traumatized women of color
don't need to tell you their story and explain
their traumas to you, just so you can understand
why your unleashed, unfamiliar dog
running up to them is not okay,
or neighborly.

But really, what is freedom
when fear lurks right outside?
Reminding you day in and day out
that no matter what they say,
you don't belong, and
they'll do what they can to show you.
The twisted tale as old as time.
That picture-perfect power move
that always puts them ahead of you.
Because let's be real;
between me and Karen from the block,
who are they going to believe?

Y Vos Quién Sos

My identity is my deepest secret
A mystery slowly unraveled by time
Desperation for belonging
Free from isolation and shame
Bound by centuries of falsehood
Deflection   Erasure
They say that there are no Black people in El Salvador
That "colocha" is something to taunt
A slur
Had I been born with my father's hair
Would I be more lost
Wandering in the fog
Looking for the light that will make me divine
Make me loved
Or would I be in community
Unafraid to profess my love for my dark skin
For the colochos that bounce as I walk this madre earth
unapologetic and free
Certain of who I am because I "look the part"
I *feel* it
But what does it even mean to "look" Salvadoreña?
Society invalidates me and my people, my country
                    My country invalidates me and my roots

My history
Erased
They say that there are no Black people in El Salvador
Look closely, look farther
It's in our history
In our blood
In my skin
In my heart
Though I am my mother's daughter
I, too, am my father's child
A legacy I despise
and reject
Not because he's El Negro y yo su Negrita
Pero porque me abandonó cuando lo amaba más
My lifeline to my past
My history
My roots
lost when he walked away

Genetic Fear

I imagine death so much it feels more like a memory.
Since before I was born I've had death looming over me.
Media muerta and born to survivors bred to survive,
but I never got a chance to tell my parents
I just want to thrive!

The oligarchs who massacred Indigenous innocents.
Fourteen families who ordered and slayed
freedom fighters opposing their oppression,
mis ancestros queridos y desconocidos.

Mami was born in 1948
in one of the departamentos
where La Matanza took place.
Sonsonate, El Salvador 1932,
not that long ago too.

U.S. occupation, bloodshed and greed.
Twelve years of war, numerous border crossings,
and a fight and flight to safety in unknown stolen land.

The memories of the fallen build the fabric of my DNA,
their loss is my legacy.
Trauma is inherited and it lives in my blood.

Never Forget

This land is your land, no matter what they say.
Build a community of survivors and amplify our truth.
Our lineage carries on through your fire and rites.
Your words and your fight leading us to a future so bright.

My child, survivor of horror and plight,
fear not the devil and the evil they claim.
No good will come from the anger you retain.
Speak love and bring together those of us who've been silenced,
vanquished through time, trial, and prejudicial error.
Silenced no more, awakened with ancestral fervor.

You're not alone, my love, and you never will be again.
Lean onto those who carry your pain.
It's not your own to hold, and together, the burden feels light.

You carry our trauma and you carry our fight.
Divine Spirit of the lands ravaged by greed.
This is your destiny, mija, remembering with all of your might
poner una puña en la espalda de nuestro dolor.
Atender las heridas que el tiempo dejó.
Las de adentro, más profundas de las de afuera.
The scars tell the story, and yours has only just begun

Cipota Mechuda

Long, wild, and untamed
Waves flowing
like the playas
of Acajutla
With roots as deep
and dark
as our history

The volume of your ancestors' cries
Bounce and project
from your long, luscious locks
Telling a story
that's never been told
A secret buried
            under the sand for generations
until the tide began to ebb
and the truth began   to flow

You see it in your skin
                    your face
You hear it in the heckles
of the diaspora
And from the pícaros en la calle
Divesting from reality
Creating a palatable self

A reflection of idolized
colonial beauty
Hair straightened
Weight lost
Less time in the sun
Prioritizing a language
of bondage and hate
Losing your history
Silencing the ancestral cries
Your story is now
your deepest secret
The story of your ancestors
washed away
Forgotten and denied by the majority
        a prerequisite for assimilation

*"How can you be Black if there are no Black people where we come
from?"*
"You're lucky you got that good hair."

In the same breath calling him
Negro colocho
Negro desgraciado
Negro jediondo
Negrita como tu tata

The body remembers
The soul understands
And the weight of it all on my shoulders
A tangled web of distorted truths and rejection
Cut and dyed
to mask the pain
Tamed
Muted
Hidden
and no longer
forgotten

Don't Tell Me

Past
Present
Future
Woven together
creating endless streams
of beautiful blackness
Flowing into a mosaic
of splendor and despair
Intertwining with
Indigenous
glory

Atlantic meets Pacific
creating and coexisting
a culture of joy and resistance
defying the impossible

So don't tell me there aren't any Black people in El Salvador

Mi querida Prudencia will tell you otherwise
and las cumbias proclaim
nunca faltan los mirones como tú y los demás
because when you look like this
A walking reflection of your ancestor's pride
people can't help but ask
what are you?

As if short of divine isn't enough
As if surviving genocide
does not denote me
the right to be seen
as *who*
rather than
what (am I?)

Fíjate que te confundes
porque parezco de aquí y de allá
con mi pelo suelto o trenzado
La gente de dos tierras
ascending before your eyes
Don't tell me there aren't any Black people in El Salvador
Porque mira no mas aquí estoy
The only begotten lovechild
of El Negro y su Nena
Negrita, toda crecida

and they didn't call me that for nothing so
Don't tell me there aren't any Black people in El Salvador
when I'm standing right here

Sibling Strife

He had a funny way of showing emotions.
His love for me
hurt me,
hit me,
broke me.

He talked shit to me,
        about me,
                and the like.

                        (That saying about words never hurting
                                didn't apply to his.)

Having daughters changes a man.

He did.

Enough for me to love, hate, and forgive.
This ceaseless cycle of emotions churning my heart into bloody pieces.
I gulp them down

one
      by
            one.

The tiny morsels of my fears find themselves coalescing cautiously
to a near-perfect form of incomplete wholeness.
It never is

whole.

It's amazing what the love of a daughter can do.
Gracias a Dios they never met the man I once knew.

The fists that once rained down upon my dark skies
embraced those girls with love and warmth like the sunshine,
his personal form of forgiveness.
(He swears he's really trying this time.)

Lo vi desde lejos, en la misma manera que lo puedo querer.

I miss him
more as a father to his girls
than anything else.

Parachute

Anger comes forth before the fall,
the silence breaks you faster than the impact.
There's no one to blame but yourself.
Only trust will set you free.
Who will be there to catch you?

Spoons

Living with chronic pain/illness my entire life, I didn't always have the vocabulary or experience to describe to others what living in my body is like. There is a lot of stigma and shame in having an "invisible disability". Often folx just assumed I'm lazy along with other such descriptors when in reality, I'm literally hurting myself just to be enough.

Spoons (noun)

1. A system of measurement, organization and understanding of physiological exertion
2. How I know when I can continue or move
forward with my day
3. The number of tasks I can accomplish with the weary chronically aching body that carries me through the world

One for waking up
Another for getting out of bed
Bonus spoon for brushing your teeth
and washing your face

Grocery shopping requires a surplus of spoons
Think *Costco party-pack for a quinceañera*
Pack of spoons
Navigating aisles

Festered with the slow flow of moving bodies
Taking up space unaware of their
malignant imposition
Dodging pedestrian traffic and shopping carts
as you race to reach the last rotisserie chicken
because after this
you won't have the spoons
to cook any of the nourishing meals
you spent three spoons trying to plan

Some days you wake up and feel like
a mahogany box full of golden spoons

laid with mother of pearl
        jade and obsidian
The power of this earthly energy
coursing through
your body
a force to be reckoned
Immovable
and stunningly fierce

Most days
(Today)
You find an old rusted spoon
buried in the deepest pockets
of your mind
You spit polish it clean
Your sweat and tears bringing it to a glisten
and you scoop out what little you have left of yourself
Serving up a delightful facade
of wellness and ability
Most take for granted
(and know you so well for)
because

For so long
This was the only spoon
you've used
The one that fed
the lies of your condition
One mouthful at a time
to all the discerning eaters
who pick and dine
on your energy
and the love that you scrape
        from the bottom of yourself
with very little left
for you to enjoy

A Love Letter to the White Women At My Last (and every) PWI

And while my body holds the trauma
keeps the score of your indifference
my ancestors mend
and tend the wounds in my heart

I impart upon you
A most generous offering
Because sharing is caring and
all I know to do is hold you dear and near
so here you go
A sliver of my pain
gift wrapped in iron and gold
buried deep in the recesses of your body
Untouchable and immovable

May it wake you in the depths of night
Shaken and afraid
cold sweat sticking to your sheets
Disrupting your rest
Like a pebble in your shoe
blistering and cutting deep into your soul

May the fear and unworthiness
you bestowed upon me
ascend from my body and placed onto yours
manifest the reality of your shame
with every blink of your eyes

May your disregard for my humanity
be all you feel until
you have no choice but to
step down from the tower of power and lies
your privileged alabaster self is ill-equipped to lead

May no one else endure
your performative self-serving ego
and see the truth behind
your complicit lies

A destiny you've manifested
for you and yours
While I and mine still struggle to survive
the structures of your kind

May you never shake me off
Remembering
my name, my face, my pain
with every person of color
who steps in and dips out
because they see in you
what I refused to see
The truth in who you are
The gatekeepers of our survival
A predator in plain sight

Afterlife

What worlds await beyond this earthly plane.
We are here divided by time and space.
Bound by love and blood,
gratitude overflows, and in it lies
the complexities of our past.

We have loved, we have lost,
we have grown, and we have fought
for all that is ours and all that was taken.

The place I once called home
is but an echo in a distant memory
waiting to vanish into the ether
like the words of my past,
and the dreams of my ancestors
sealed in eternity.

A Constitution for the UnForgotten

Preamble:
We hold these truths to be self-evident;

We were not, in fact, created equal.

But instead have tipped the scales,

overpowering the white lie
passed from generation to generation,
tightening the hold that binds justice blind.

They call it a conquest, yet here We stand,
still surviving the vitriol they spit upon our native land.

Two histories divided and intertwined,
the story of our struggle and our rise combined.
A destructive disconnection unmerited.
Drunk on broken dreams and ancient promises inherited.

A blessing and a curse full of pride and contempt,
coiled in conflict and mired with oppressive attempts.
We, the people of this land, survivors of the taken
proclaim these words for the ones forsaken.

May we never forget them...

La Declaración

We who do not forget
the power coursing through us,
radiating the golden flames of our past.
Illuminating the path to liberation,
igniting a blazing trail of remembrance,
clearing the way for the lil' homies
who hold and mold our sacred future.

Our future rooted in tradition, growing tall
with the power of matriarchal magic
and radical remembrance.
We who do not forget las mujeres de maíz,
porque sin nosotras no hay país.
Nosotras cargando la sangre y el agua,
las palabras que conectan rama y raíz.
Toma esta tortilla, nuestro pan de cada día.
The sacred body grown from
the unforgotten seeds of amor y agonía.

Toma y bebe, drink from my cup that overflows.
Imbibing the blessed blood that cleanses and overthrows.
The fear washed down, purified by their sacred brew,
their raucous roistering laughter rippling through.
Rejoice! Let the celebration roll off your tongue.
Disfruta la abundancia de nuestro ser,
y recuerda que la parranda's just begun.

Singing songs of freedom on full blast,
those canciones de recuerdo que bailan en el aire.
A ceremony of recollection and reclamation.
Whispering wisdom and sensations from beyond,
transcribed into these shaky rhymes and songs
amplified high to heaven, where the ancestors cry in glee,
raining blessings down on We who do not forget.

El Camino

I've been finding my way back home
since I came to understand
what it means to be and live in diaspora.
Following the breadcrumbs left behind,
the aftermath of our attempted destruction.

Trying to find my way back,
burrowing deep into my psyche.
Celebration and joy be the markers
where my memories come to life.
Balloons in the air soaring into great unknowns,
leading me back to the playground of my past.
Pulling that distant power into my present,
letting it take me away to that special place
where laughter and glee are the background track
to my oh-so gloomy days.

Home is a place I've only seen in pictures and
the faint memories of a childhood lost.
The dreams that awaken me with smiles and cold sweat,
the waters from a land we once called home
for millennia before the story we all know.
I come from people of the land,
                    air, and the sea.
The salt of the ocean seasoning our souls,
the skin on our hands blessing
the bounty of all that we touch.
The earth beneath our sacred feet
blooming a path for us to follow.
A trail of blood, sweat, and
tears trailing behind
our 500-year march.
Looking,
longing, yearning
for home.

FIN

Endings
are but a drop of water in the ocean
the ripples traveling
far and wide
connecting and moving
those in its wake

Endings
scaffold and bleed
into beginnings that we
may never see
Not fearing what comes after
only what we leave
behind

Remembering
that we celebrate our
timeless connection blessed by
the earth and sea
to which one day
I and we
will return

My words
forever in the ether
on the pages of books
in libraries
I will never see
In the hands of people
I will never meet and
in the hearts of
other
healing souls
hoping for a future
I too
thought
I'd never see

Aknowledgements

This book could not have been possible without the monumental support of my loves near and far. My family, chosen and by blood, the communities, and kin that have shaped me, held me and always believed in me, even when I didn't.

To my three angels, Mami, Joey y Menche, para todos los ancestros que me crearon y los que nunca conocí. Gracias por siempre cuidar, guiar y alimentar mi alma y ser.

My family, all the cousins, the elders, ancestors, and especially the young ones I've held and helped raise (even from afar), y'all are my guiding light, my beacons of hope, and my wildest dreams come true. I couldn't be more grateful for the blood and love we share.

My seestur Katie, my ride or die and survivor of our history, I'm grateful for the love and time we've been blessed with. I'm grateful for you still being here with me during these times of change and unrest. We're in this together, and together we thrive.

To my Tio. For all the books, the lessons, and laughs- you're the only man in my life that means more to me than a father ever could. Thank you for gifting me The Stories of Eva Luna all those years ago. I still remember the day, and I still have that tattered copy with me, along with the passion and love of reading and writing that grew from that one moment.

To Jason for gifting me with the time and space to heal and reflect. Thank you for being the best quarantine buddy I could ever ask for. I love you.

My Alegria fam, the comadres and comrades that encouraged me to be brave and believe in my power, there are not enough words for the gratitude and love that fills my heart when I think of you. All of you.

To Davina, my mentor and literary-fairy godmother, I can't even begin to express how much your support and encouragement have helped me during this time. You taught me the importance of getting out of my comfort zone and my own way. Without you, this book and this moment in my life would not be possible. Thank you from the bottom of my heart.

To the Duwamish and Coast Salish people, the original stewards of the land where these words came together, I hope that with this message, more will fight for your recognition and rights. May we pay our respects and our reparations to you at RealRentDuwamish.com

To Andi and Dania, y'all are the love and community I needed, and it only took me 4 years in the PNW and 300 miles to find y'all. And it was all worth it.

My Texas family, y'all...I miss you every day, and there isn't a moment where I don't wish I could have Fufu, Karaoke, and coffee with y'all. Thank you for making me feel whole and at home when it was just me and the world. I wouldn't be where I am today without your love and lasting friendship.

To Dr. Heather for being the container and healer to the deep wounds I held hidden for so long. Thank you for reminding me that my words are medicine that can one day heal others.

My lil homie, cohost and friend for life, Melody, we've been through it, in it and over it. Together, forever.

My homie josh for keeping it real and helping me through one of the most turbulent times of my life; your love and friendship are the greatest things to come out of Seattle. Thank you for helping me bring this book baby to life with your powerful wisdom and unending support.

To Jordan Alam for being an incredible inspiration, teacher, teammate and friend.

To Diea May, a love my heart and family will never forget and always hold dear. Thank you, amiga, for being you and loving me so much.

To The Most Honorable Brynn Barquise DeLafayette. You're the best thing that ever happened to me. Your unconditional love and affection have often been the only thing that has gotten me through when it felt like nothing else could.

To the high school English teachers at RHS, Botello, and Schallert, who noticed something in my words that no one ever had before. Thank you for saving my life.

To the high school homies that stuck with me through all that and more. For making it out alive. For holding each other when some of us didn't. For giving me some of my best moments during the hardest part of my life. Y'all don't even know. I love you all so.

To the publishers and publications that amplified my work; Thank you for affirming that my words are meant to be seen and heard. A very special thank you to Alegría Publishing for creating a much-needed space for Latinx writers to discover their true potential and reach farther than ever thought possible. To Valiant Scribe for your inclusion of The Tale of the Melting Pot in your Vultures and Doves edition. To The South Seattle Emerald and Marti for sharing Fuck The Fork with all of your readers. To Leisa at IndieIt for being an incredible cheerleader and giving me the time and platform to share part of my story. To Reyna y Laura of Fingir, for sharing my truth in your inaugural issue and for taking YVQS all the way to Washington D.C . To Ethan and the curators of Quiet Lighting, for bringing me into their powerful literary mixtapes and letting me share The Audacity. To @BIPOCWritingParty for holding space and challenging the creativity that rests within. For gifting me the powerful prompt of We Who Do Not Forget. I never will.

To the nonprofits that are bringing transformative change and challenging the status quo. My CJ and SeattleWorks fam, y'all are the real MVP's and every day that I breathe, I trust in the work that you bring. Y'all give me the hope I need to remember that another way IS possible.

To AFROOS, Carlos Lara, y Dr. Daniella Parada for fighting and advocating for our Afro-Salvi recognition, history, and truth. Thank you for teaching me the hidden reality of my roots and continuously working to uplift our Afro-Salvi and Indigenous communities.

To the indigenous land and water defenders across all of Abya Yala, my words can only speak a fraction of the monumental work and devotion you pour into our sacred earth. May the land continue to heal and thrive in your care. May we move into a phase of indigenous sovereignty and reclamation of our divine inheritance.

To the children of diaspora. Los diasporicos. All of us spread far and wide across the world. Those of us lost and looking, searching for connection and community. May you find home and healing in these words, and remember that you are part of something greater.

And to you, my beloved reader. I've spent my entire life searching for you, yearning to share these bittersweet truths that keep us tethered in time and blood. You are the greatness the world needs, the heart and soul of our liberation that beats with every word you feel. I'm grateful for you today and every day.

Payush

Joey Paquito José
08.04.1971-02.15.2016

Bio

Clara Olivo (she/her/ella) is an Afro-Salvi poet living in diaspora.
Born and raised in South Central L.A. to Salvadorean refugees, Clara
weaves history and lived experience, creating transcendental poetry
that amplifies ancestral power and pride.

Writing for her lost inner child, Clara steps into her poetry with
the intention of healing the hurts of her past and inspiring hope for
the future. Since finding her voice, she has performed in open mics
and art receptions from Seattle to Washington D.C., and has been
featured in publications such as *The South Seattle Emerald, Valiant
Scribe, and Quiet Lightning's Literary Mixtape.*

Clara lives in a quiet home on unceded Duwamish land with her
partner, dog, and an ever-growing number of plants. You can follow
her on Instagram @HijaDeMilagro and @TheDiasporicConnection
and become a part of her journey.